Francis Frith's
Around Falmouth

PHOTOGRAPHIC MEMORIES

Francis Frith's
AROUND FALMOUTH

Martin Dunning

First published in the United Kingdom in 1999 by
Frith Book Company Ltd

Hardback Edition 1999
ISBN 1-85937-066-7

Paperback Edition 2002
ISBN 1-85937-594-4

Reprinted in hardback 2002

British Library Cataloguing in Publication Data

Francis Frith's Around Falmouth
Martin Dunning

Frith Book Company Ltd
Frith's Barn, Teffont,
Salisbury, Wiltshire SP3 5QP
Tel: +44 (0) 1722 716 376
Email: info@francisfrith.co.uk
www.francisfrith.co.uk

Printed and bound in Great Britain

As with any historical database the Frith archive is constantly being corrected and improved and the publishers would welcome information on omissions or inaccuracies

Contents

FRANCIS FRITH: *Victorian Pioneer*

FRANCIS FRITH, Victorian founder of the world-famous photographic archive, was a complex and multitudinous man. A devout Quaker and a highly successful Victorian businessman, he was both philosophic by nature and pioneering in outlook.

By 1855 Francis Frith had already established a wholesale grocery business in Liverpool, and sold it for the astonishing sum of £200,000, which is the equivalent today of over £15,000,000. Now a multi-millionaire, he was able to indulge his passion for travel. As a child he had pored over travel books written by early explorers, and his fancy and imagination had been stirred by family holidays to the sublime mountain regions of Wales and Scotland. 'What a land of spirit-stirring and enriching scenes and places!' he had written. He was to return to these scenes of grandeur in later years to 'recapture the thousands of vivid and tender memories', but with a different purpose. Now in his thirties, and captivated by the new science of photography, Frith set out on a series of pioneering journeys to the Nile regions that occupied him from 1856 until 1860.

INTRIGUE AND ADVENTURE

He took with him on his travels a specially-designed wicker carriage that acted as both dark-room and sleeping chamber. These far-flung journeys were packed with intrigue and adventure. In his life story, written when he was sixty-three, Frith tells of being held captive by bandits, and of fighting 'an awful midnight battle to the very point of surrender with a deadly pack of hungry, wild dogs'. Sporting flowing Arab costume, Frith arrived at Akaba by camel seventy years before Lawrence, where he encountered 'desert princes and rival sheikhs, blazing with jewel-hilted swords'.

During these extraordinary adventures he was assiduously exploring the desert regions bordering the Nile and patiently recording the antiquities and peoples with his camera. He was the first photographer to venture beyond the sixth cataract. Africa was still the mysterious 'Dark Continent', and Stanley and Livingstone's historic meeting was a decade into the future. The conditions for picture taking confound belief. He laboured for hours in his wicker dark-room in the sweltering heat of the desert, while the volatile chemicals fizzed dangerously in their trays. Often he was forced to work in remote tombs and caves where conditions were cooler. Back in London he exhibited his photographs and was 'rapturously cheered' by members of the Royal Society. His reputation as a photographer was made overnight. An eminent modern historian has likened their impact on the population of the time to that on our own generation of the first photographs taken on the surface of the moon.

Venture of a Life-Time

Characteristically, Frith quickly spotted the opportunity to create a new business as a specialist publisher of photographs. He lived in an era of immense and sometimes violent change. For the poor in the early part of Victoria's reign work was a drudge and the hours long, and people had precious little free time to enjoy themselves.

Most had no transport other than a cart or gig at their disposal, and had not travelled far beyond the boundaries of their own town or village. However, by the 1870s, the railways had threaded their way across the country, and Bank Holidays and half-day Saturdays had been made obligatory by Act of Parliament. All of a sudden the ordinary working man and his family were able to enjoy days out and see a little more of the world.

With characteristic business acumen, Francis Frith foresaw that these new tourists would enjoy having souvenirs to commemorate their days out. In 1860 he married Mary Ann Rosling and set out with the intention of photographing every city, town and village in Britain. For the next thirty years he travelled the country by train and by pony and trap, producing fine photographs of seaside resorts and beauty spots that were keenly bought by millions of Victorians. These prints were painstakingly pasted into family albums and pored over during the dark nights of winter, rekindling precious memories of summer excursions.

The Rise of Frith & Co

Frith's studio was soon supplying retail shops all over the country. To meet the demand he gathered about him a small team of photographers, and published the work of independent artist-photographers of the calibre of Roger Fenton and Francis Bedford. In order to gain some understanding of the scale of Frith's business one only has to look at the catalogue issued by Frith & Co in 1886: it runs to some 670

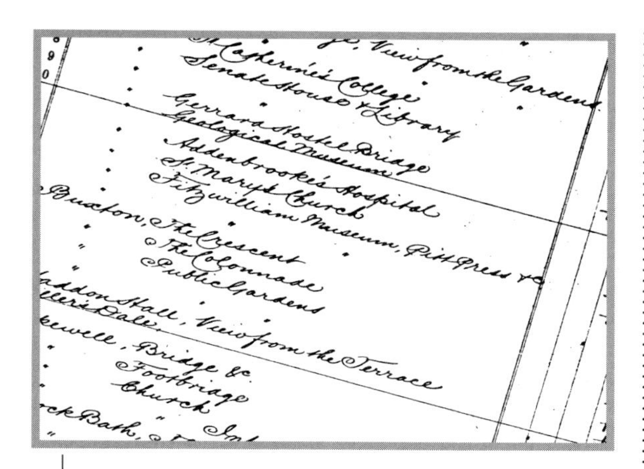
St Catherine's College, View from the Garden
Senate House & Library
Gerrard Hostel Bridge
Geological Museum
Addenbrooke's Hospital
St Mary's Church
Fitzwilliam Museum, Pitt Press &c
Buxton, The Crescent
The Colonnade
Public Gardens
addon Hall, View from the Terrace
llers Dale
kewell, Bridge &c
Footbridge
Church

pages, listing not only many thousands of views of the British Isles but also many photographs of most European countries, and China, Japan, the USA and Canada – note the sample page shown above from the hand-written *Frith & Co* ledgers detailing pictures taken. By 1890 Frith had created the greatest specialist photographic publishing company in the world, with over 2,000 outlets – more than the combined number that Boots and WH Smith have today! The picture on the right shows the *Frith & Co* display board at Ingleton in the Yorkshire Dales. Beautifully constructed with mahogany frame and gilt inserts, it could display up to a dozen local scenes.

Postcard Bonanza

The ever-popular holiday postcard we know today took many years to develop. In 1870 the Post Office issued the first plain cards, with a pre-printed stamp on one face. In 1894 they allowed other publishers' cards to be sent through the mail with an attached adhesive halfpenny stamp. Demand grew rapidly, and in 1895 a new size of postcard was permitted called the court card, but there was little room for illustration. In 1899, a year after Frith's death, a new card measuring 5.5 x 3.5 inches became the standard format, but it was not until 1902 that the divided back came into being, with address and message on one face and a full-size illustration on the other. *Frith & Co* were in the vanguard of postcard development, and Frith's sons Eustace and Cyril continued their father's monumental task, expanding the number of views offered to the public and recording more and more places in Britain, as the coasts and countryside were opened up to mass travel.

Francis Frith died in 1898 at his villa in Cannes, his great project still growing. The archive he created continued in business for another seventy years. By 1970 it contained over a third of a million pictures of 7,000 cities, towns and villages. The massive photographic record Frith has left to us stands as a living monument to a special and very remarkable man.

Frith's Archive: *A Unique Legacy*

Francis Frith's legacy to us today is of immense significance and value, for the magnificent archive of evocative photographs he created provides a unique record of change in 7,000 cities, towns and villages throughout Britain over a century and more. Frith and his fellow studio photographers revisited locations many times down the years to update their views, compiling for us an enthralling and colourful pageant of British life and character.

We tend to think of Frith's sepia views of Britain as nostalgic, for most of us use them to conjure up memories of places in our own lives with which we have family associations. It often makes us forget that to Francis Frith they were records of daily life as it was actually being lived in the cities, towns and villages of his day. The Victorian age was one of great and often bewildering change for ordinary people, and though the pictures evoke an impression of slower times, life was as busy and hectic as it is today.

See Frith at www.francisfrith.co.uk

We are fortunate that Frith was a photographer of the people, dedicated to recording the minutiae of everyday life. For it is this sheer wealth of visual data, the painstaking chronicle of changes in dress, transport, street layouts, buildings, housing, engineering and landscape that captivates us so much today. His remarkable images offer us a powerful link with the past and with the lives of our ancestors.

Today's Technology

Computers have now made it possible for Frith's many thousands of images to be accessed almost instantly. In the Frith archive today, each photograph is carefully 'digitised' then stored on a CD Rom. Frith archivists can locate a single photograph amongst thousands within seconds. Views can be catalogued and sorted under a variety of categories of place and content to the immediate benefit of researchers. Inexpensive reference prints can be created for them at the touch of a mouse button, and a wide range of books and other printed materials assembled and published for a wider, more general readership - in the next twelve months over a hundred Frith local history titles will be published! The day-to-day workings of the archive are very different from how they were in Francis Frith's time: imagine the herculean task of sorting through eleven tons of glass negatives as Frith had to do to locate a particular sequence of pictures! Yet the archive still prides itself on maintaining the same high standards of excellence laid down by Francis Frith, including the painstaking cataloguing and indexing of every view.

It is curious to reflect on how the internet now allows researchers in America and elsewhere greater instant access to the archive than Frith himself ever enjoyed. Many thousands of individual views can be called up on screen within seconds on one of the Frith internet sites, enabling people living continents away to revisit the streets of their ancestral home town, or view places in Britain where they have enjoyed holidays. Many overseas researchers welcome the chance to view special theme selections, such as transport, sports, costume and ancient monuments.

We are certain that Francis Frith would have heartily approved of these modern developments, for he himself was always working at the very limits of Victorian photographic technology.

The Value of the Archive Today

Because of the benefits brought by the computer, Frith's images are increasingly studied by social historians, by researchers into genealogy and ancestory, by architects, town planners, and by teachers and schoolchildren involved in local history projects. In addition, the archive offers every one of us a unique opportunity to examine the places where we and our families have lived and worked down the years. Immensely successful in Frith's own era, the archive is now, a century and more on, entering a new phase of popularity.

The Past in Tune with the Future

Historians consider the Francis Frith Collection to be of prime national importance. It is the only archive of its kind remaining in private ownership and has been valued at a million pounds. However, this figure is now rapidly increasing as digital technology enables more and more people around the world to enjoy its benefits.

Francis Frith's archive is now housed in an historic timber barn in the beautiful village of Teffont in Wiltshire. Its founder would not recognize the archive office as it is today. In place of the many thousands of dusty boxes containing glass plate negatives and an all-pervading odour of photographic chemicals, there are now ranks of computer screens. He would be amazed to watch his images travelling round the world at unimaginable speeds through network and internet lines.

The archive's future is both bright and exciting. Francis Frith, with his unshakeable belief in making photographs available to the greatest number of people, would undoubtedly approve of what is being done today with his lifetime's work. His photographs, depicting our shared past, are now bringing pleasure and enlightenment to millions around the world a century and more after his death.

FALMOUTH – *An Introduction*

FALMOUTH LIES at the mouth of an estuary into which flow seven rivers, two of which - the Penryn River and the Truro River - are navigable for some distance inland to important Cornish towns. To the south-west is the great bulk of the Lizard, taking the sting out of the prevailing south-westerlies that roar in from the Atlantic, and adjacent to the town itself is the rampart of Pendennis Point, an ideal lookout which also serves as a natural breakwater.

Given its commanding position, it is perhaps surprising that no major settlement existed on Falmouth's site before the 17th century. Penryn (founded in 1216) and Truro both pre-date Falmouth by hundreds of years; indeed, there is a local rhyme that goes 'Penryn was a flourishing town, when Falmouth was a furzy down'. Penryn and Truro were both inland and therefore safer from any raiders than Falmouth-to-be, and by Tudor times the River Fal was busier than any other port in the land. Henry VIII recognised the importance of the estuary and fortified both Pendennis Point and its opposite number at St Mawes, but it was not until the reign of Henry's daughter, Elizabeth I, that Falmouth really began to grow, reputedly at the suggestion of Sir Walter Raleigh.

A small port and community called Pennycome-quick had existed for some time, serving Arwenack House, the home of the Killigrews, and it was this family who were to be the true founders of Falmouth. Sir John Killigrew (also the first Governor of Pendennis Castle) developed the little port until his death in 1584. His descendants (confusingly all called John for the next three generations) carried on his work, interspersed with odd bouts of piracy, and sometime around the end of the 16th century or the beginning of the 17th, Sir Walter Raleigh stayed at Arwenack House and convinced the then Sir John of the potential of Falmouth. In 1613, Falmouth was well and truly founded by Sir John Killigrew, to the sound of much objection from the good people of Penryn and Truro, who foresaw their cosy little monopoly on trade being broken.

During the Civil War, Cornwall was fiercely Royalist; Sir John Killigrew defended Arwenack gallantly before it was finally burnt down, and the garrison at Pendennis under Sir John Arundel held out for five months against the Parliamentarian forces. Despite this resistance, the Killigrews seem to have been looked on favourably by Cromwell, for they were still powerful and wealthy at the Restoration of the Monarchy in 1660; King Charles II, doubtless remembering their support for his father, granted the town its charter in 1661. A little before this the Customs post had moved from Penryn to Falmouth, and it seemed that the gloomy predictions of Penryn and Truro were being borne out.

In 1688, Falmouth received an important boost, both for its trade and status - the arrival of the Packets. The Post Office decided that the port was to be the base for its mail boats - fast brigantines of about 200 tons that could outrun almost anything else on the water, and frequently did just that. As well as mail they carried passengers and small, expensive cargoes such as bullion; their captains and crew had immunity from Customs searches and boosted their earnings with 'Free Trading', the name by which generations of Cornishmen have sought to give respectability to smuggling. In their heyday more than 40 'Falmouth Packets' (after which the local newspaper is still named) plied their rapid trade to Europe and the Americas from Falmouth.

The Packets needed supplies and repairs, and their crew and passengers needed places to stay; thus two of the industries that Falmouth still relies upon - ship repairs and hotels - came into being. The Greenbank Hotel was built for Packet passengers and New Quay at Flushing was the victualling depot.

Wars were fought. Trade flourished in this commodity and waned in that; new religious movements, such as Methodism, sprung up, disease reared its head and people were born, married and buried. And through it all, the ships came and went, and Falmouth prospered and grew on its precious maritime lifeblood.

But not all mariners were engaged in legal endeavours. During the 18th century, smuggling became probably the most important industry in Cornwall. It had been practised for hundreds of years, of course - in Elizabethan times 75% of the tin produced in Cornwall was smuggled out to avoid coinage duties - but a combination of the loss of markets through war and punitive import duties resulted in dire poverty and the rise of 'free trading'. One observer estimated that in 1800 over 40,000 people were directly involved in Cornish smuggling. Many more were indirectly involved; priests, the gentry, MPs, JPs and even Customs men connived or turned a blind eye, while the presence just inland of a large community of hard-drinking miners ensured a warm welcome for rum, gin and especially brandy, or 'cousin jackie', of which 9,000 gallons was seized in September 1762 alone. Tea, tobacco, snuff and wool were smuggled as well as spirits, brought ashore in the remote coves and creeks of the Lizard, the Helford River and the Fal.

The loss to the public purse was causing consternation at the Treasury, however, and once Napoleon had been dealt with, a determined effort was made to stamp out free trading. A coastal blockade was enforced in 1820 which eventually became the Coastguard service in 1829. The abolition of some of the duties and a growing temperance movement, combined with the blockade, made things more difficult for the smugglers; by 1835 trade had declined to a fraction of what it had been, although a few die-hards carried on and doubtless do so today.

Falmouth's growth continued, however. As the town grew, so did the fishing fleet and the number of ships visiting to discharge cargo or await orders. Greenbank Terrace was built by Georgian sea captains, and a thriving shipbuilding and repair industry took root. The Packets were moved to Southampton in 1842, amid much protest, but the people of the town, ever resourceful, looked elsewhere for business. In 1858 the burghers of Falmouth engaged one James Abernethy, an engineer, leased 150 acres of land, and formed the Falmouth Docks Company.

The passing of the Falmouth Docks Act in 1859, and the arrival of the railway a few years later, ensured the success of the venture. Ship repairs were the main business, but cargo ships brought in corn and coal and took on board china clay, stone and salted pilchards for export. Ships called for orders at the rate of 20 a week, providing business for the victuallers and chandlers, and Falmouth continued to thrive.

During World War I the docks were temporarily taken over by the Admiralty. Falmouth lost only six ships of the 58 convoys that sailed from the port to enemy action. By comparison, the Second World War was rather more eventful. The newly extended docks worked at full capacity dealing with convoy casualties, and Carrick Roads rarely had fewer than 100 vessels anchored. Both the docks and the town were bombed in 12 raids and 31 people killed. The St Nazaire raid, which led indirectly to the sinking of the Bismark by depriving her of a home port, was organised at Falmouth, and in 1944 the Docks were a major embarkation point for the D-Day landings in Normandy.

The eyes of the world turned to Falmouth in 1952 when the salvage tug Turmoil went to the aid of the freighter Flying Enterprise in a storm 300 miles out in the Atlantic. The epic rescue attempt, which ended 60 miles from safety in a final dramatic jump from the funnel of the sinking ship by Captain Kurt Carlsen and Kenneth Dancy, mate of the Turmoil, were followed by anxious radio listeners the world over.

Robin Knox-Johnstone chose Falmouth

for his first single-handed non-stop voyage round the world in his little yacht Suhaili. On landfall in 1969 he was asked by a rather straight-laced Customs official where he had sailed from: 'Falmouth!' he replied. Behind the dramas, the life of the port went on. Fish were caught (although the pilchard stocks were in steep decline), the tugs busied themselves like sheepdogs nipping and nudging their charges into and out of the busy docks and, with the advent of cheap motor transport and more leisure time, tourists flocked to the county.

Today, Falmouth remains a maritime town, albeit with a rather different emphasis than in the past. The docks employ a fraction of the 3,000 people who worked there in the late fifties, and the fishing fleet is suffering, like fleets everywhere, from the depletion of the stocks. The surrounding rivers and creeks are busier than ever before with vessels, but the whispers of the smugglers and the sound of muffled oars have been replaced by the chug of diesels at weekends and during the summer, when local people take their boats out for pleasure rather than business.

For most, cars have replaced boats as the conveyance by which they carry out their business, but should you be in Falmouth and want to get to Flushing, or across to St Mawes, a ferry trip is still the quickest way to travel. And everywhere in this small gem of a Cornish town, even down to the name of the local newspaper, are reminders of Falmouth's proud maritime history.

Ships, Docks and Ferries

WHEN Sir John Killigrew started developing the embryonic port of Falmouth in the 16th century, he can hardly have imagined how the harbour was going to look by the end of the 20th century. To walk today along the whole of Falmouth's waterfront, from the quay at the Greenbank Hotel to the end of the Eastern Breakwater, is a fair step of almost six miles, although the actual distance along the curving shore of the inner harbour is a mere two miles.

Passing North Quay and Customs House Quay, Sir John and his 17th century descendants would have felt at home, for they have changed little; but as they travelled eastwards and reached the docks area with its railway terminus and miles of piers and basins, they would have thought they were in another world. And what would they have made of the enormous Queen Elizabeth Dry Dock, built in 1958? The dock is 850 feet long, 136 feet wide and its building involved the removal of some 300,000 cubic yards of rubble. What use could there possibly be for such an enormous hole in the ground? We are used to giants of the sea, of course - tankers are the length of three football pitches, so vast that the crew often use bicycles to get from one end to the other - but in Sir John's day, ships like Sir Francis Drake's Golden Hind were mere minnows, no more than 120 feet long and weighing perhaps 3-400 tons. Faced with 100,000 tons of tanker, Sir Walter Raleigh, fine seaman though he undoubtedly was, would have been left scratching his head as to where to moor it. This is no problem for the modern port, however, although vessels any bigger are limited to anchoring in the bay. This inability to deal with the real behemoths of the ocean, plus stiff competition from the likes of Korea and Japan, nearly dealt a death blow to the docks in the seventies - an echo, several hundred years later, of how the development of Falmouth affected the trade of Truro and Penryn.

In Sir John Killigrew's time, any ship falling foul of the treacherous weather of the Western Approaches was on her own and faced the added problem, should she run aground on the rocks of the Lizard, of locals exercising wreckers' rights and stripping the wreck of everything of value. Today, HM Coastguard Falmouth manages shipping for a vast area, and radio, radar and satellite navigation have made the mariner's trade a more precise science and far safer. Should a vessel get into trouble, the nearby Royal Naval Air Station at Culdrose can fly helicopter missions far out into the Atlantic, while one of the salvage tugs stationed in the Carrick Roads battles its way through the storm and the brave men of the lifeboat crew stand by. Sir John might feel a little surprised at the way his brainchild has grown.

Market Strand 1890 24208

Market Strand pier was built in 1871 from granite at the astronomical cost of £1,732. Moored at the quay is the St Mawes Ferry, either the 'Roseland' or the 'Queen of the Fal'. In the background are the docks, now thirty years into their life and still growing.

The Pier 1890 24208a

The Prince of Wales, later to become King George V, laid the foundation stone of the extension to this pier in 1903. Alongside is the St Mawes Ferry. On the opposite bank are only a few houses; today the shore is developed as far as Kilnquay Wood in the centre of the picture.

THE LANDING STAGE 1904 53032
In 1859 an Act of Parliament enabled the building of the docks. In 1860 the first stone was laid, and the arrival of the Great Western Railway in 1863 allowed quick and easy handling of cargoes. Imports included coal and phosphates, while china clay and pilchards were exported.

THE JETTY 1904 53033
This photograph shows the rivalry of steam versus sail. At this time, sail was still competing with steam because of lower fuel costs, but crew's wages and the unpredictability of service due to the vagaries of the wind meant that the writing was on the wall.

THE FISHING FLEET 1910 62889
For centuries the staple diet of Cornwall's coastal communities was pilchards. Failure of the pilchard catch could mean starvation: when this happened in Fowey in the 1780s the population lived for months on limpets prised from the rocks at low tide. Fishing smacks came to fish Falmouth's waters from as far afield as Lowestoft.

The Harbour 1918 68779
In the foreground is the tug 'Victor' departing laden with passengers for Church Cove. It was owned by Captain W Thomas.

The Pier c1960 F4135
The pier is undergoing repairs: the wooden sheds of previous pictures have been replaced by more substantial concrete structures, and there is now a shelter at the end for ferry passengers. The St Mawes Ferry is still alongside, now powered by diesel rather then steam.

62 FH

THE HARBOUR 1908 61058
On the beach is a fishing lugger typical of the East cornish type. These have a transom stern instead of a pointed stern.

MARINE HOTE

The Quay 1908 61059
This area of the Quay was built by Sir Peter Killigrew in the 1670s. The picture shows a fleet of fishing luggers and, in the background, the tower of the Parish Church of King Charles the Martyr, one of only five churches of that name in the country.

PENDENNIS HEAD FROM TREFUSIS 1895 37042
This picture shows well how the great bulk of Pendennis Head shelters Falmouth harbour and docks from the savage south-westerly winds that prevail in Cornwall. In the foreground is one of Falmouth's famous quay punts, the workhorses of the busy port.

THE HARBOUR 1895 37047
This photograph, probably taken from Customs House Quay, shows just how busy the harbour was. The quay punts are seen here for the most part at anchor, with only their mizzen sails rigged. They took supplies and water to visiting ships, brought the ships' crews ashore for recreation, and on their days off competed fiercely and with much pride in races.

THE 'CUTTY SARK' 1924
One of Britain's most famous ships, the 'Cutty Sark' made her first voyage in 1870; she plied a distinguished trade for many years before she fell on hard times. She was rescued by Captain W H Dowman of Trevissome, and brought to Falmouth in 1924 as a training ship.

THE HARBOUR 1930
Taken from Trefusis, this photograph shows the 'Cutty Sark' still at anchor. Later she was reconditioned and moved to her permanent home in Greenwich. Just right of centre on the horizon is the Falmouth Hotel, and to its left is Pendennis Head.

THE 'CUTTY SARK' 1924 76614

THE HARBOUR 1930 83153

THE 'IMPLACABLE' 1927 80103

THE 'IMPLACABLE' 1927

HMS 'Implacable' was originally built for the French Navy in 1789 and fought at Trafalgar as the 'Duguay Trouin'. Captured, she found her way to Falmouth in 1912, and was used as a holiday ship for boys. Older residents of Falmouth still remember hearing the bugle from the decks first thing in the morning.

THE HARBOUR AND THE 'CUTTY SARK' 1930

By 1930, shipbuilding had ceased in Falmouth, but the docks still flourished. The majority of ships were now steam, and fuelled from oil bunkers at the 8,500 ton storage 'farm' built in 1924 near the Eastern Breakwater.

THE HARBOUR AND THE 'CUTTY SARK' 1930 83155

Town Quay c1960 F4144
This photograph is taken from Customs House Quay. The little harbour is still full of working boats, but the modern equivalent of the quay punt no longer has sails, but a diesel engine.

The Harbour c 1960 F4181
The docks have welcomed ships from all nations and carrying every imaginable cargo. Because of its oil storage capacity of up to 30,000 tons, it used to see many tankers of up to 100,000 tons in the harbour and 250,000 tons anchored offshore.

THE HARBOUR c1960 F4183

THE HARBOUR c1960
These harbour tugs spent their working days shepherding ships into and out of the docks. There is usually a large ocean-going salvage tug anchored in the estuary ready to go to the aid of any ship in distress out in the English Channel.

CUSTOMS HOUSE QUAY c1960
Falmouth's Customs House was built in the late 17th century when HM Customs moved from Penryn. The prominent chimney, known as 'the pipe', was used for the burning of contraband tobacco seized by the revenue men.

CUSTOMS HOUSE QUAY c1960 F4191

Town and Church

STANDING on the Moor, the fine open space behind Market Strand, with its Town Hall and library and bustling with buses and cars, your feet are standing on relatively new ground, for this was once marsh and a small creek - Smithwick ('Smith's village') Creek. Indeed, there is still an area of the town by that name.

Another one of the settlements that was to grow into modern Falmouth was Penny-come-quick. The name is in fact a corruption of the Cornish 'Pen-y-cuik', meaning the head of the creek, and is not as unusual as you might imagine - Plymouth too has an area with this curious name at the head of Stonehouse Creek. Arwenack Manor, the estate which these settlements served, was burned down during the civil war, but its walls remained as ruins for many years and have recently been renovated.

No settlement can really consider itself a town until it has a church, of course. Penryn had one in 1265 - the church and college at Glasney, which met its end at the time of the dissolution of the monasteries - but Falmouth had to wait. In 1661 King Charles II granted Sir Peter Killigrew the town's charter on condition that a church was built and dedicated to his father: King and Martyr. It is one of only five churches so named in the country. It was completed in 1664, consecrated by the Bishop of Exeter in 1665, and the first rector was the Rev Francis Bedford. The living of the rector of Falmouth became a wealthy one. Under the Act of Parliament of 1664, all houses and shops were obliged to pay a rate of 16 pence in the pound to the Rector.

Another act required every decked ship to pay the Rector port duties of sixpence on entering the port, in return for which the Rector had to keep a pole and flag erected to mark the Black Rock in the harbour. By Victorian times, the living was worth £10,000 annually - a considerable sum.

At the time of the Charter, Falmouth consisted of some 400 houses. With the arrival of the Packet service, the town really took off, easily outstripping Penryn as a port. Much of the building that went on was in some way associated with the sea. The fine Georgian houses of Greenbank Terrace were built as the homes of retired sea captains; the Greenbank Hotel took advantage of Packet passengers; Marlborough House was built by Packet commander Captain John Bull and named after his ship the 'Duke of Marlborough'; and the arrival of the railway was integral to the development of both the docks and the holiday business. Today, Falmouth's population numbers nearly 20,000, a figure that swells considerably during the tourist season. It is a vastly different place from the two old settlements of Smithwick and Penny-come-quick.

The Green Bank Hotel 1890 24209
At this time, before the advent of the car, the main road into Falmouth from Penryn was still unmetalled. The Green Bank Hotel was built in 1785 to accommodate passengers for the Packets, which often anchored off Flushing (in the background).

THE GREEN BANK HOTEL 1930 83156
The road is now metalled and the car has arrived. It was from the Green Bank Hotel that Kenneth Grahame wrote letters to his son starting 'My Darling Mouse' - letters that would eventually become the much loved children's classic 'The Wind in the Willows'.

VIEW FROM FLUSHING 1890 24213
The fine Georgian terrace visible on the riverfront is Green Bank Terrace, the final port of call for the retired sea captains who built the houses. The Green Bank Hotel can be seen above the quay on the right.

Green Bank Terrace from Flushing 1895 37041
Only five years on, Falmouth has grown, most obviously in the right of the picture. At this time the docks were flourishing, with 5-600 tons of cargo unloaded every day and 20 vessels a week visiting the estuary .

View from Wellington Terrace 1890 24203
The sunlit, imposing building at the centre is the Town Hall, built in 1864 and dominating the open square of The Moor. On the left is the long, low Old Market, and on the opposite side of the Penryn River the small fishing village of Flushing.

View from the Observatory 1890 24204
The Bowling Green at the top of Trelawney Road has long since become a playground. The long roof in the foreground is that of Albert Cottages. In the background the Penryn River curves inland to the port of Penryn, which lost so much trade to its growing neighbour.

THE TOWN CENTRE C1960 F4098
Gone is the old low market building, replaced by the Passmore Edwards Building and, on the far left, the Post Office. The prominent tower is the clock tower of the old Board School. The school was bombed during the war and the tower was pulled down in the 1960s.

FOX'S LANE 1908 61056
The tree-lined Fox's Lane runs from Wood Lane to Melville Road. Too narrow for cars, it remains much the same today as it did in 1908.

The Manor House 1904
Arwenack House was the ancestral home of the Killigrew family. Sir John Killigrew was responsible for starting the development of Falmouth as a port before his death in 1584, and Sir Peter Killigrew built the parish church of King Charles the Martyr in 1662.

Arwenack Avenue 1904
Arwenack Avenue, known to the Killigrews as the 'Long Walk', still has at its north end the gate posts of the old Arwenack estate. Its length and straightness meant that it was at one time covered and used as a rope walk for spinning hemp.

The Manor House 1904 52229

Arwenack Avenue 1904 52229a

THE MOOR 1903 50518
In the centre is the Town Hall and to its left the Passmore Edwards Building, built in 1894 and containing the library, rates office, and the Mayor's Parlour. Passmore Edwards was a rich philanthropist, and buildings all over Cornwall and South Devon bear his name. The obelisk is a memorial to the Packetsmen, unveiled in 1898 at a parade led by the men of HMS 'Ganges'.

CHURCH STREET c1960 F4095
Taken from the forecourt of the Church of King Charles the Martyr, this shows one of the narrow main streets of the town.

Market Street c1960 F4103
The Woolworth's building (centre left) now stands on the site of the old Baptist chapel. On the right are the premises of Clarke & Co, Gentleman's Outfitters.

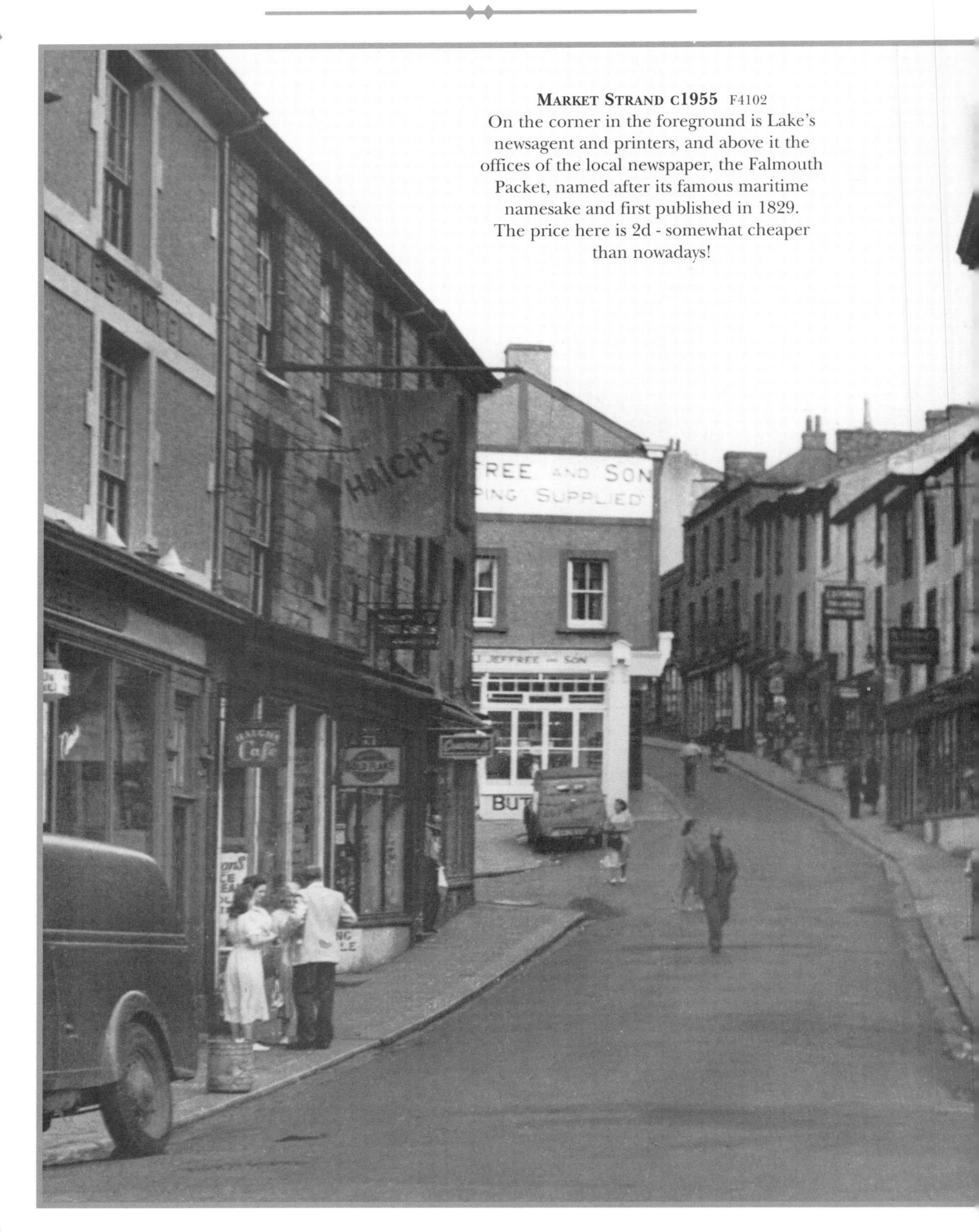

MARKET STRAND c1955 F4102
On the corner in the foreground is Lake's newsagent and printers, and above it the offices of the local newspaper, the Falmouth Packet, named after its famous maritime namesake and first published in 1829. The price here is 2d - somewhat cheaper than nowadays!

OFFICES OF
Falmouth Packet
ESTABLISHED 1829
BEST FOR NEWS
FOR ADVERTISING
LARGEST LOCAL SALE
Fridays 2d
PRINTERS.

MARKET STRAND c1960 F4106

The prominent turret on the left belongs to the King's Hotel. In the left foreground is West End Department Store, Drapery and Furnishings, opened by a Mr Sarah and first managed by Mr Porter.

ARWENACK STREET c1960 F4094

Arwenack Street maintains much of its character today, although local businesses have to some extent been replaced by national chains. In 1960 the chains had yet to make their presence felt, and small business were the order of the day. Note the interesting dual usage of the building on the left - both shipping office and chemist.

The Town Centre c1960 F4120
Taken from Berkeley Vale and looking down the East side of the Moor, this view shows at left the Town Hall and on the right the imposing edifice of Wesley Methodist Church, bombed during World War Two and subsequently rebuilt.

The Parish Church 1918 68792
The parish church of King Charles the Martyr was built as a condition of the town being granted its charter by Charles II in 1661. It has an unusual rectangular tower and, rarely for this country, bells played by a carillon.

THE CHAPEL OF GYLLYNGDUNNE HOUSE 1930 83160
Gyllyngdunne House was at one time home of the Rector of Falmouth; this was reputed to be his private chapel, but was in fact never consecrated and was probably only a summer house. In the last century the living of Falmouth was one of the richest in the south-west with an annual income of £10,000!

The Observatory c1960 F4256
The Observatory on Western Terrace was used for many years for making meteorological records - note the anemometer on the roof - and is now a residential home.

The Bowling Green Post Office c1960 F4279
Marlborough Road leads down from the Post Office to Clare Terrace and the National Primary School. In the foreground on the left is the old-style school warning sign - a torch representing knowledge.

Around the Estuary

TO TRAVEL from St Anthony's Lighthouse to Pendennis Point round the shore of the entire Fal estuary, with all its creeks and inlets, is a journey of well over fifty miles. Seven rivers and countless smaller streams flow into the great sheltered anchorage of the Carrick Roads, which runs north from Falmouth for four miles.

The Percuil River, with the picturesque village of St Mawes at its mouth, runs north for a few miles through the Roseland peninsula; from the head of its estuary a journey of less than a mile westwards leads back to the shore of the Carrick Roads at the equally beautiful village of St Just-in-Roseland.

Further up the Fal, round the corner from Turnaware Point and past the looming bulk of two merchantmen anchored and mothballed, is the King Harry Ferry, an essential service which considerably shortens the road journey from one side of the estuary to the other. The source of the Fal itself is over twenty miles away up on the bleak expanse of Goss Moor.

The most northerly point of the estuary is on the Tresillian River, a place much-loved by smugglers in times past. Three miles west is Cornwall's capital, Truro, once an important port but now visited mainly by pleasure boats, and south is the village of Malpas with its foot ferries. Further south down the western side of the estuary are Cowlands Creek and Trelissick, built at the north end of the Carrick Roads in the mid-18th century by Captain John Lawrence and one of Cornwall's finest houses. Restronguet Creek, just south of Feock, runs inland to Devoran, a busy mining port in the middle of the last century. Down the shore again is Mylor Creek, which for some years had the distinction of being the navy's smallest dockyard.

Trefusis Point, opposite Falmouth, and a popular spot over the centuries for a Sunday afternoon picnic, is at the mouth of the Penryn River, on whose north shore lies Flushing, home to the packet captains and crews. Round the headland, or more easily reached by crossing the narrow peninsula that joins Pendennis to the mainland, are Falmouth's holiday beaches, Gyllyngvase and Swanpool, and further south on the coast of Falmouth Bay is the delightful little cove of Maen Porth.

South again, past the bulk of Rosemullion Head, is the mouth of the Helford River. Like the Fal Estuary it is heavily wooded and has plenty of mysterious and tranquil creeks. Although only five miles as the crow flies from Falmouth, to get to St-Anthony-in-Meneage on the southern shore of the Helford River requires a road journey of twenty miles.

A glance at the map reveals the existence of at least six ferries on the estuary of the Fal - ferries that are still very much in use to link what are still isolated communities. The stretch of water between Flushing and Greenbank was known as 'King's Roads'; a literal interpretation of this name, along with Carrick Roads, reveals the importance of the waterways of the Fal in the life of local communities, for although great natural barriers, they have for centuries been the 'roads' which have allowed life to prosper.

St Anthony's Lighthouse 1890 24222
Sixty-five feet high and visible for 13 miles, the lighthouse was built in 1834-5 by Trinity House to indicate the entrance to the estuary of the Fal. Opposite is Pendennis Head with its castle visible on the skyline.

St Mawes Castle 1910 62884
St Mawes, like Pendennis built by Henry VIII, guards the eastern entrance to the estuary. However, it was built on a less than well-chosen site and during the Civil War soon fell when besieged by Parliamentarian forces, unlike Pendennis which held out for five months.

St Mawes
1890 24229
The sheltered little harbour of St Mawes, east across the Carrick Roads from Falmouth, was once a busy fishing port. It has changed relatively little, but now the boats are mostly pleasure craft and the population largely retired.

St Mawes
1890 24232
In 1890 the harbourside was still cobbled; few vehicles came here, as the main access was still by water and the village was quite isolated. The cart in the foreground would have offered a rather uncomfortable ride, with its iron-shod wheels striking sparks from the cobbles. The hillside in the background is nowadays quite built up.

ST MAWES, FISHERMEN'S COTTAGES 1890 24236

ST MAWES
Fishermen's Cottages 1890

The life of a Cornish fisherman may seem romantic, and their dwellings picturesque, but take a closer look at these dilapidated fishermen's cottages with their broken windows. In reality the life of a fisherman was hard and dangerous, and when the stocks failed, the result was grinding poverty.

KING HARRY FERRY c1960

The King Harry Ferry crosses the river at Trelissick, five miles inland from Falmouth. King Harry Passage is mentioned as early as 1649, but the steam ferry did not operate until 1889. It takes its name from the chapel dedicated to Our Lady and King Henry that once stood on the Tolverne side.

KING HARRY FERRY c1960 F4211

MALPAS AND THE RIVER FAL 1895 37063
Eight miles inland from Falmouth, the tiny village of Malpas is situated at the junction of the Truro River (which takes the valley in the centre right) and the River Fal, in the right foreground. The arm of the Fal in the top left of the photograph leads to Falmouth and the sea.

MALPAS AND THE RIVER FAL 1895 37065
Much of the land around Malpas is owned by Lord Falmouth. As a result, the village has changed little and looks much the same today. The River Fal leads right out of the picture up to Tregothnan, Lord Falmouth's ancestral home.

MALPAS FERRY AND THE RIVER FAL 1895 37067

MALPAS FERRY AND THE RIVER FAL 1895
Malpas, situated on a point at the junction of the Truro and Tresillian Rivers, actually has three ferries. In 1895 they would have been rowing boats like those in the picture; today, the ferrymen's arms and backs are spared by the advent of the diesel engine.

DEVORAN C1955
Devoran, at the mouth of the Carnon River, was a backwater until 1820 when the mineral railway arrived, bringing tin and copper down the Carnon Valley and carrying coal back to power the mine engines and pumps.

DEVORAN C1955 D120001

DEVORAN, THE VILLAGE c1955 D120010
1845-65 were Devoran's boom years, with up to 30 ships in port at any one time and five trains a day. By 1870 the mines were in decline, and within a few years the dock was empty and the railway gone. Devoran's fine terraces remain, however, as a reminder of more prosperous times.

MYLOR c1960 F4115
The tiny village of Mylor, in the next valley north of the Penryn River, has one of the oldest bridges in the area, built in 1590. Mylor was once the site of the smallest Royal Naval dockyard in the land.

COWLANDS CREEK, RIVER FAL 1912 64749
The tiny hamlet of Cowlands, at the head of a creek just above the King Harry ferry, is only a couple of miles south of Truro, but feels isolated and remote even today. Little creeks such as this were much frequented by smugglers.

FLUSHING, TREFUSIS FIELDS 1918 68789
Trefusis Fields to the west of Flushing are still a popular picnic spot, reached by a ferry journey of a few minutes from Falmouth Pier. In Edwardian times it was common for whole families to row across from Falmouth for a Sunday afternoon out.

FLUSHING 1918 68783
Flushing, north from Falmouth across the stretch of water known as 'Greenbank Road', was a centre for the masters and crews of the packets before the service moved to Southampton. New Quay was used for victualling the packets.

FLUSHING, FROM GREEN BANK 1893 31843
The tiny village of Flushing, on the opposite bank of the Penryn River from Falmouth, remains relatively unchanged today except in one important respect. Just after World War Two you could buy a cottage there for £400, but today it would cost you perhaps two hundred times as much!

PENRYN, THE CHURCH 1904 53052
The now-defunct Glasney College was founded in Penryn to train men for the priesthood as far back as 1264 by Bishop Bronescombe. The church of St Gluvias was consecrated in 1318, although the oldest parts existing date from the 15th century.

Penryn, The Church Institute 1897 39501
The building to the right of the Swan Inn is rather unusual for Penryn in that it is not built of granite. It was recorded in 1577 that, apart from St Ives, no town in Cornwall had more wine houses or pubs than Penryn.

Penryn 1897 39499
Penryn's later prosperity came from its granite quarries. In 1840 John Freeman came to the area and soon there were over 60 Freeman quarries, exporting stone all over the world. The Old Bailey, New Scotland Yard and Fastnet Rock Lighthouse are all built of Penryn granite.

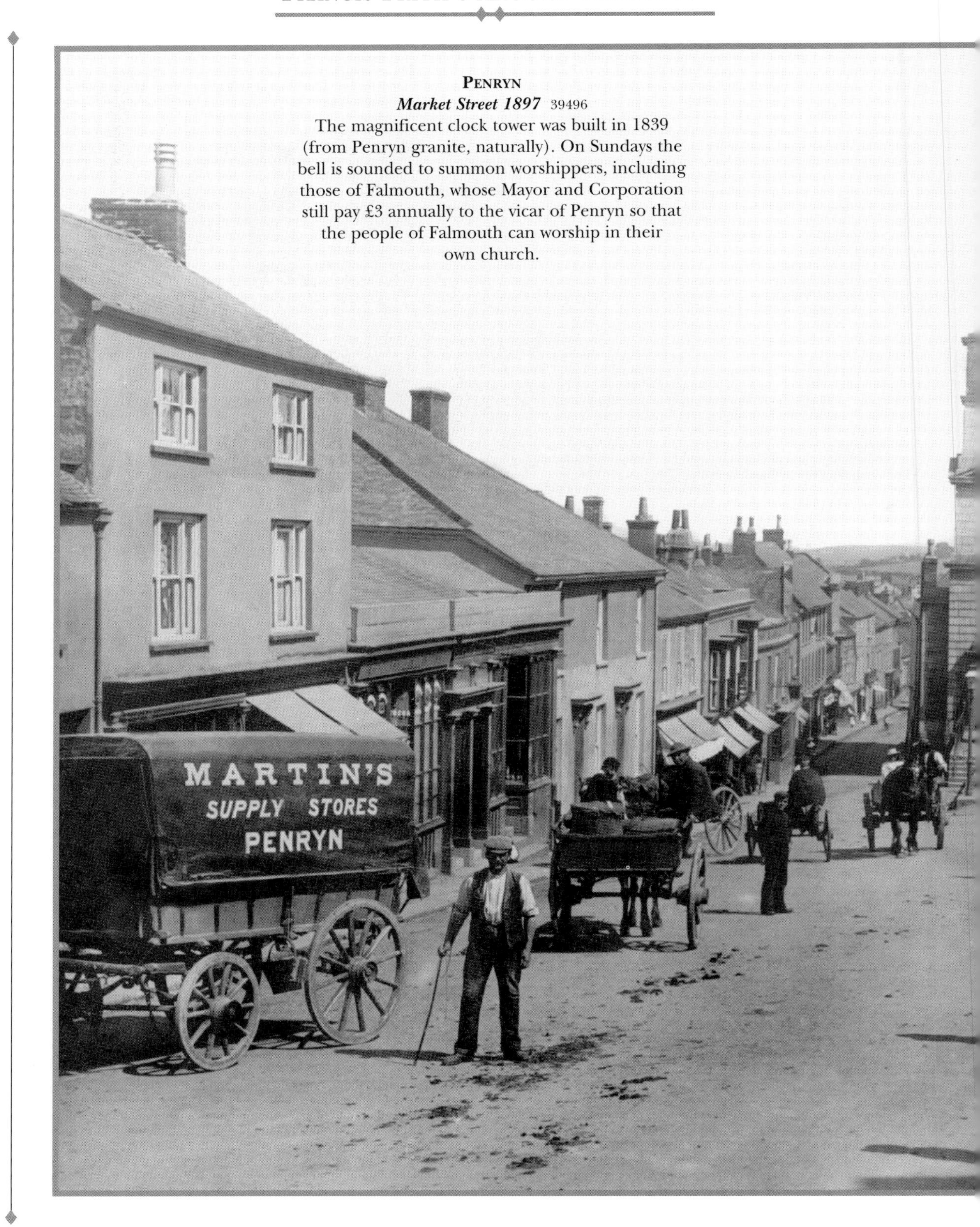

PENRYN

Market Street 1897 39496

The magnificent clock tower was built in 1839 (from Penryn granite, naturally). On Sundays the bell is sounded to summon worshippers, including those of Falmouth, whose Mayor and Corporation still pay £3 annually to the vicar of Penryn so that the people of Falmouth can worship in their own church.

HAIR CUTTING
SHAVING
ROOMS

PENRYN, STREET SCENE 1890 27650

On the night of 12 April 1862, 30 houses were destroyed and 400 made homeless by a fire that required three engines to extinguish it - two from Penryn itself, and one that was specially landed from HMS 'Russell'. Perhaps the group of men in the centre are descendants of those earlier firemen.

Pendennis Castle 1890

Pendennis Castle was built by Henry VIII to guard the entrance to Carrick Roads, thereby protecting the important ports of Penryn and Truro. It was beseiged in 1646 when Parliamentary forces attacked the fortress from both land and sea. The garrison held out for six months before finally surrendering. At the end they were forced to eat dog and horse meat to survive.

Swanpool Beach 1903

Swanpool Beach, to the west of Falmouth, was much frequented by smugglers during the 18th century. French cognac, or 'Cousin Jackie', was the biggest cargo, and in the 1770s it was estimated that 469,000 gallons a year was being smuggled - a quarter of it into Cornwall.

Pendennis Castle 1890 24227

Swanpool Beach 1903 50521

SWANPOOL BEACH 1930 83161
In the distance to the right is the Falmouth Hotel and in the foreground is the celebrated painter Henry Tuke's studio. Swanpool Beach (far left) is a sandy bar dividing Swan Pool from the sea. The area behind Swanpool Beach was once mined for lead and silver.

SWAN POOL 1910 62880
Swan Pool, so named for obvious reasons, is a lake behind the sand bar of Swanpool Beach. It was very popular for racing model yachts. Up the valley today is Swanvale, a suburb originally built in the 1920s to house engineering workers from the rapidly expanding docks.

Marlborough Farm 1908 61054
This road leads down through Swanvale to Swan Pool. Marlborough Farm, parts of which still stand, was the home farm for Marlborough House, named after the 'Duke of Marlborough', one of the Royal Mail Packets skippered by Captain John Bull, who built the house.

PENNANCE 1908 61050
This house on the clifftop is Wilkins Cottage, long since demolished. The track above the house leads out to Pennance Head, with its wooded crest.

MAENPORTH BEACH 1904 53032a
This secluded, sandy little cove lies two miles down the coast from Falmouth. The large house in the woods at the top of the hill is Crag House, later converted to become the Crag Hotel, which burned down some years ago.

Mawnan, The Church c1955 M202002
The name of the 13th-century church of St Mawnan still defies interpretation; nobody is sure who Mawnan was. The church sits on the hill 150 feet above Parsons Beach at the mouth of the Helford River, isolated from the community it serves.

Mawnan, The Coastline c1955 M202001
Looking north, the first cove (hidden behind the house centre left) is Bream Cove. Maenporth is hidden behind the next headland, and beyond (centre right) is Pennance Point. In the far distance is the hazy outline of Pendennis.

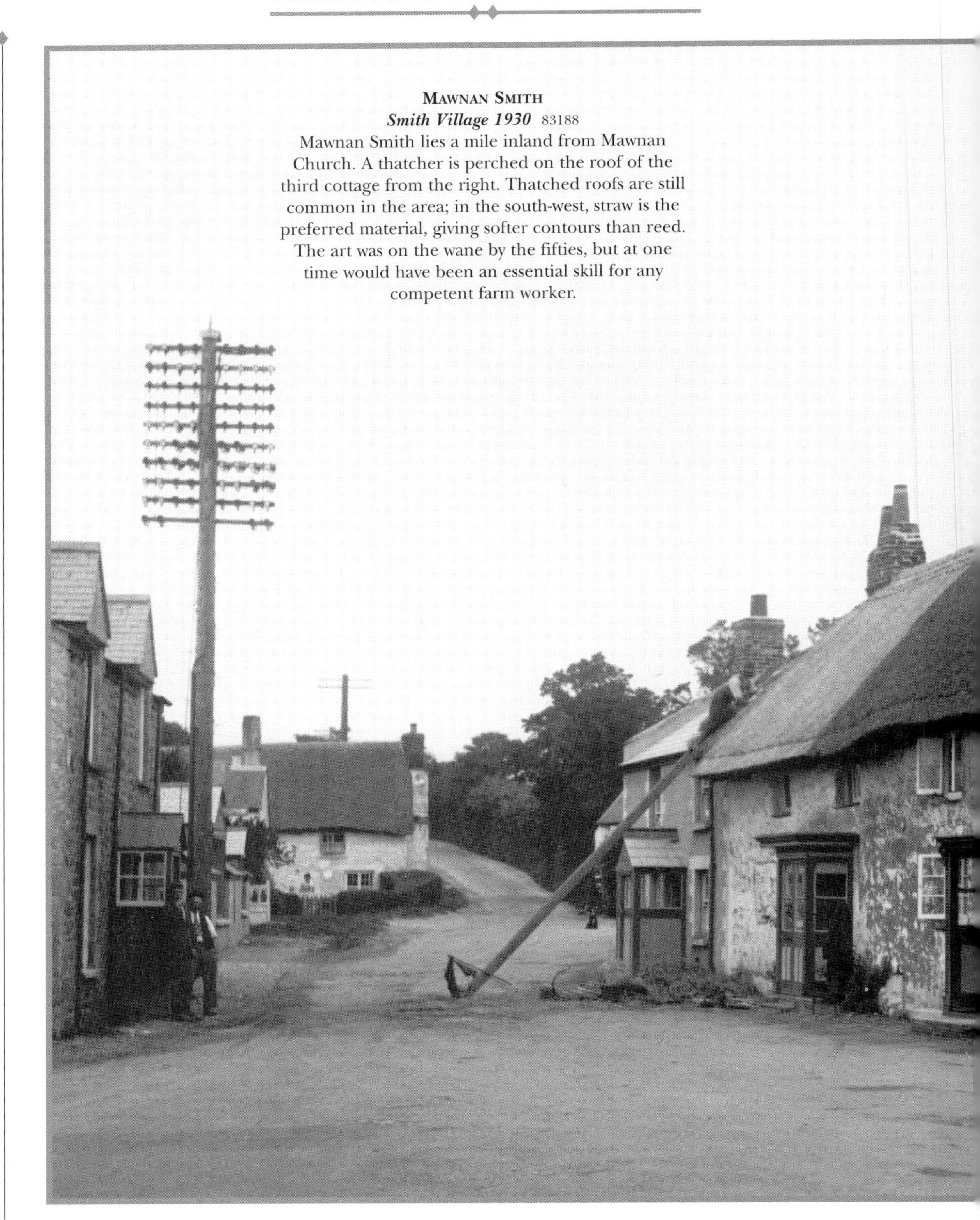

Mawnan Smith

Smith Village 1930 83188

Mawnan Smith lies a mile inland from Mawnan Church. A thatcher is perched on the roof of the third cottage from the right. Thatched roofs are still common in the area; in the south-west, straw is the preferred material, giving softer contours than reed. The art was on the wane by the fifties, but at one time would have been an essential skill for any competent farm worker.

COCHRANE

MAWNAN SMITH, SMITH VILLAGE 1930 83190
The Red Lion Inn still sits on the junction at the centre of Mawnan Smith. The road on the left leads down to Parson's Beach and St Mawnan Church, while that on the right goes to Helford Passage and the ferry across the Helford River.

HELFORD PASSAGE c1960 F4292
Helford Passage, on the north bank of the Helford River, is the departure point for the foot ferry to Helford Village. Today it is considerably more built up.

Constantine, The Old Town c1955 C408003
Lying just north of Polwheveral Creek (an easterly tributary of the Helford River), Constantine was at one time surrounded by working granite quarries, from where came the stone for its fine terraces - and for the original Waterloo Bridge in London.

Constantine, The Post Office c1955 C408002
Not all Cornish roads are narrow and bendy; fine wide streets and pavements are not uncommon in Cornish towns. Constantine has changed little since this picture was taken, although the little boy in the background would need to keep his eye open for traffic were he to stand in the middle of the road to buy his ice cream today.

THE HELFORD RIVER 1890 24244
Remote and beautiful, the Helford River was a favoured haunt of smugglers who used the cover of its heavily wooded coves and creeks to bring their contraband ashore away from the ever-vigilant eyes of the Revenue men.

WEAR HELFORD 1890 24245
The village of Helford, a couple of miles up the Helford River, is the picture of what a Cornish village should be. The next creek upriver from Helford is the fabled Frenchman's Creek, location of Daphne du Maurier's novel of the love between a landed lady and a French pirate.

The Seafront

THE FINE beaches of Falmouth's southern shore have not always been the preserve of ice cream vans and children digging feverishly with buckets and spades.

Before the advent of Cornwall's tourist trade, they were more likely to be frequented by locals in search of food - fish, crabs, or in really hard times limpets scraped from the rocks - or by smugglers bringing contraband ashore.

The opening of the railway from Truro to Falmouth in 1863 alerted the attention of a shrewd consortium of local businessmen to the potential of the hotel trade. It had originally been intended that the new railway station should be at Greenbank, but the decision to make the docks the terminus gave the chance to build a hotel with sea views, and so the Falmouth Hotel was born. Opened in 1865, it had its own landing stage on the small beach in front of the hotel. Business prospered and more hotels followed, among them the Pendennis Hotel, built in 1893 by the Falmouth Hotel Company. The Gyllyngdune Estate prevented the sea-front road being completed in a westerly direction until 1903, when the council bought the estate from F J Horniman, the local MP.

Development eastward was held up by a reluctance on the part of the Falmouth Hotel Company to lose their private access to the beach. A narrow pedestrian walkway known as Invalid's Walk was the only access between Cliff Road and Castle Drive until 1908. Then, with the help of John Barker MP, the hotel company was at last prevailed upon to sell the land to the Corporation. The new road was opened on 31 July 1908 by the Rt Hon R B Haldane, HM Secretary of State for War, who apparently used his opening speech as a recruiting drive for the armed forces! One elderly resident still recalls being wheeled in her pram by her grandfather across the road before it was opened.

There now existed a magnificent drive from the harbour all the way round Pendennis Point to Gyllyngvase Beach; other hotels took advantage of the situation, including the Bay Hotel, and pavilions were built to enable visitors to appreciate the sea air without being too exposed to the undesirable effects of the sun. Queen Mary Gardens appeared in 1910. Falmouth's relatively balmy climate allowed the growth of exotic plants, and although they have the appearance of palm trees the characteristic Dracaenae are not true palms - one has to go to Torquay for that!

Hotels, as is their nature, have come and gone over the years - the Bay Hotel site now holds flats - but people still flock to the town year on year to enjoy the climate and the magnificent views south and east that can be seen from Falmouth's sea front.

From Pendennis Castle 1890 24196
The large building centre left is the Falmouth Hotel, built in 1863 after the railway had arrived and local businessmen had realised the town's potential as a resort. It was across this narrow peninsula that Parliamentary forces under Colonel Fortescue threw a cordon during the siege of Pendennis in 1646.

FROM PENDENNIS 1895 37032

A mere five years on, the hotels have extended westward from the Falmouth Hotel along Gyllyngvase Beach towards Swanpool Point; construction of Cliff Road is under way, although it still has some way to go before it extends, as it does today, all the way out to Pendennis.

FROM PENDENNIS 1897 40596B

Guests at Falmouth's hotels cannot always enjoy the fine beaches, as this stormy view shows. The grounds of the Falmouth Hotel were the site in World War 2 of an underground shelter. A direct hit on it by a bomb killed several US servicemen and their girlfriends.

Marine Drive 1908 61039
The coast road has been finished under the supervision of Mr Tresidder, the Town Surveyor, and it is now possible to walk or drive all the way from Gyllyngvase Beach around Pendennis Head and back into Falmouth.

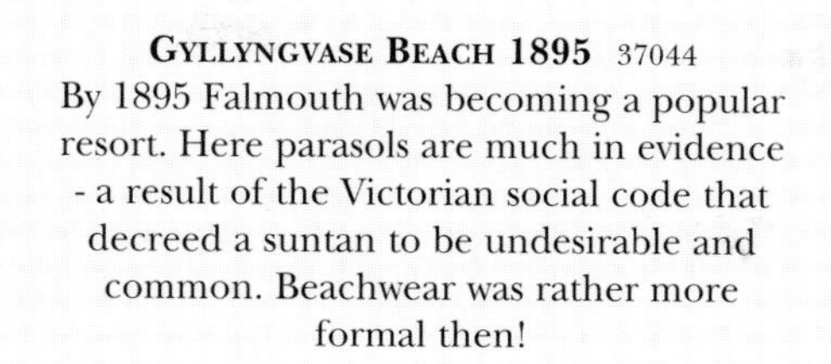

GYLLYNGVASE BEACH 1895 37044
By 1895 Falmouth was becoming a popular resort. Here parasols are much in evidence - a result of the Victorian social code that decreed a suntan to be undesirable and common. Beachwear was rather more formal then!

The Sands 1908 61047
Almost exactly the same view of Gyllyngvase Beach, but thirteen years on and not a parasol in sight. The Edwardians obviously had a more relaxed policy on suntans, although everybody is still wearing hats.

INVALID'S WALK 1908 61042
Once Cliff Road had been built it became a popular promenade spot. Running beneath it is Invalid's Walk, often frequented by visitors to the local Hydro, who had come to take the waters. In the far distance on the right is St Anthony lighthouse.

CASTLE BEACH C1960 F4337
A very low tide with the rocks exposed. Not quite the swinging sixties yet (apparently they did not get under way until 1963) but beach etiquette and dress codes have largely been discarded. The Victorians would not have approved.

Gyllyngvase Beach, St Vincent's Anchor 1908 61048
This enormous anchor came from HMS 'St Vincent', broken up in Falmouth Docks in 1906. It was taken away for scrap during World War Two.

THE BAY HOTEL 1908 61065a
Recently demolished to make way for a block of flats, the Bay Hotel was built in 1909 by the Falmouth Hotel Company on Cliff Road. On the right is the Pavilion, built for sitting and taking the sun, while in the foreground are the steps that lead down to the beach.

THE FALMOUTH HOTEL c1960 F4361
The impressive Victorian edifice of the Falmouth Hotel, built in 1863, was only actually half completed. The second stage, a mirror image of the first which was intended to be added on later at the far end, was never built.

QUEEN MARY GARDENS c1960 F4364
The gardens were built in 1910 by popular demand on the site of a stinking marsh. The land was given by Lord Kimberley, and the money for the project by the wife of the local MP.

Index

Around the Estuary

Frith Book Co Titles

www.francisfrith.co.uk

The Frith Book Company publishes over 100 new titles each year. A selection of those currently available are listed below. For latest catalogue please contact Frith Book Co.

Town Books 96 pages, approx 100 photos. County and Themed Books 128 pages, approx 150 photos (unless specified). All titles hardback laminated case and jacket except those indicated pb (paperback)

Amersham, Chesham & Rickmansworth (pb)	1-85937-340-2	£9.99
Ancient Monuments & Stone Circles	1-85937-143-4	£17.99
Aylesbury (pb)	1-85937-227-9	£9.99
Bakewell	1-85937-113-2	£12.99
Barnstaple (pb)	1-85937-300-3	£9.99
Bath (pb)	1-85937419-0	£9.99
Bedford (pb)	1-85937-205-8	£9.99
Berkshire (pb)	1-85937-191-4	£9.99
Berkshire Churches	1-85937-170-1	£17.99
Blackpool (pb)	1-85937-382-8	£9.99
Bognor Regis (pb)	1-85937-431-x	£9.99
Bournemouth	1-85937-067-5	£12.99
Bradford (pb)	1-85937-204-x	£9.99
Brighton & Hove(pb)	1-85937-192-2	£8.99
Bristol (pb)	1-85937-264-3	£9.99
British Life A Century Ago (pb)	1-85937-213-9	£9.99
Buckinghamshire (pb)	1-85937-200-7	£9.99
Camberley (pb)	1-85937-222-8	£9.99
Cambridge (pb)	1-85937-422-0	£9.99
Cambridgeshire (pb)	1-85937-420-4	£9.99
Canals & Waterways (pb)	1-85937-291-0	£9.99
Canterbury Cathedral (pb)	1-85937-179-5	£9.99
Cardiff (pb)	1-85937-093-4	£9.99
Carmarthenshire	1-85937-216-3	£14.99
Chelmsford (pb)	1-85937-310-0	£9.99
Cheltenham (pb)	1-85937-095-0	£9.99
Cheshire (pb)	1-85937-271-6	£9.99
Chester	1-85937-090-x	£12.99
Chesterfield	1-85937-378-x	£9.99
Chichester (pb)	1-85937-228-7	£9.99
Colchester (pb)	1-85937-188-4	£8.99
Cornish Coast	1-85937-163-9	£14.99
Cornwall (pb)	1-85937-229-5	£9.99
Cornwall Living Memories	1-85937-248-1	£14.99
Cotswolds (pb)	1-85937-230-9	£9.99
Cotswolds Living Memories	1-85937-255-4	£14.99
County Durham	1-85937-123-x	£14.99
Croydon Living Memories	1-85937-162-0	£9.99
Cumbria	1-85937-101-9	£14.99
Dartmoor	1-85937-145-0	£14.99
Derby (pb)	1-85937-367-4	£9.99
Derbyshire (pb)	1-85937-196-5	£9.99
Devon (pb)	1-85937-297-x	£9.99
Dorset (pb)	1-85937-269-4	£9.99
Dorset Churches	1-85937-172-8	£17.99
Dorset Coast (pb)	1-85937-299-6	£9.99
Dorset Living Memories	1-85937-210-4	£14.99
Down the Severn	1-85937-118-3	£14.99
Down the Thames (pb)	1-85937-278-3	£9.99
Down the Trent	1-85937-311-9	£14.99
Dublin (pb)	1-85937-231-7	£9.99
East Anglia (pb)	1-85937-265-1	£9.99
East London	1-85937-080-2	£14.99
East Sussex	1-85937-130-2	£14.99
Eastbourne	1-85937-061-6	£12.99
Edinburgh (pb)	1-85937-193-0	£8.99
England in the 1880s	1-85937-331-3	£17.99
English Castles (pb)	1-85937-434-4	£9.99
English Country Houses	1-85937-161-2	£17.99
Essex (pb)	1-85937-270-8	£9.99
Exeter	1-85937-126-4	£12.99
Exmoor	1-85937-132-9	£14.99
Falmouth	1-85937-066-7	£12.99
Folkestone (pb)	1-85937-124-8	£9.99
Glasgow (pb)	1-85937-190-6	£9.99
Gloucestershire	1-85937-102-7	£14.99
Great Yarmouth (pb)	1-85937-426-3	£9.99
Greater Manchester (pb)	1-85937-266-x	£9.99
Guildford (pb)	1-85937-410-7	£9.99
Hampshire (pb)	1-85937-279-1	£9.99
Hampshire Churches (pb)	1-85937-207-4	£9.99
Harrogate	1-85937-423-9	£9.99
Hastings & Bexhill (pb)	1-85937-131-0	£9.99
Heart of Lancashire (pb)	1-85937-197-3	£9.99
Helston (pb)	1-85937-214-7	£9.99
Hereford (pb)	1-85937-175-2	£9.99
Herefordshire	1-85937-174-4	£14.99
Hertfordshire (pb)	1-85937-247-3	£9.99
Horsham (pb)	1-85937-432-8	£9.99
Humberside	1-85937-215-5	£14.99
Hythe, Romney Marsh & Ashford	1-85937-256-2	£9.99

Available from your local bookshop or from the publisher

Frith Book Co Titles (continued)

Title	ISBN	Price
Ipswich (pb)	1-85937-424-7	£9.99
Ireland (pb)	1-85937-181-7	£9.99
Isle of Man (pb)	1-85937-268-6	£9.99
Isles of Scilly	1-85937-136-1	£14.99
Isle of Wight (pb)	1-85937-429-8	£9.99
Isle of Wight Living Memories	1-85937-304-6	£14.99
Kent (pb)	1-85937-189-2	£9.99
Kent Living Memories	1-85937-125-6	£14.99
Lake District (pb)	1-85937-275-9	£9.99
Lancaster, Morecambe & Heysham (pb)	1-85937-233-3	£9.99
Leeds (pb)	1-85937-202-3	£9.99
Leicester	1-85937-073-x	£12.99
Leicestershire (pb)	1-85937-185-x	£9.99
Lincolnshire (pb)	1-85937-433-6	£9.99
Liverpool & Merseyside (pb)	1-85937-234-1	£9.99
London (pb)	1-85937-183-3	£9.99
Ludlow (pb)	1-85937-176-0	£9.99
Luton (pb)	1-85937-235-x	£9.99
Maidstone	1-85937-056-x	£14.99
Manchester (pb)	1-85937-198-1	£9.99
Middlesex	1-85937-158-2	£14.99
New Forest	1-85937-128-0	£14.99
Newark (pb)	1-85937-366-6	£9.99
Newport, Wales (pb)	1-85937-258-9	£9.99
Newquay (pb)	1-85937-421-2	£9.99
Norfolk (pb)	1-85937-195-7	£9.99
Norfolk Living Memories	1-85937-217-1	£14.99
Northamptonshire	1-85937-150-7	£14.99
Northumberland Tyne & Wear (pb)	1-85937-281-3	£9.99
North Devon Coast	1-85937-146-9	£14.99
North Devon Living Memories	1-85937-261-9	£14.99
North London	1-85937-206-6	£14.99
North Wales (pb)	1-85937-298-8	£9.99
North Yorkshire (pb)	1-85937-236-8	£9.99
Norwich (pb)	1-85937-194-9	£8.99
Nottingham (pb)	1-85937-324-0	£9.99
Nottinghamshire (pb)	1-85937-187-6	£9.99
Oxford (pb)	1-85937-411-5	£9.99
Oxfordshire (pb)	1-85937-430-1	£9.99
Peak District (pb)	1-85937-280-5	£9.99
Penzance	1-85937-069-1	£12.99
Peterborough (pb)	1-85937-219-8	£9.99
Piers	1-85937-237-6	£17.99
Plymouth	1-85937-119-1	£12.99
Poole & Sandbanks (pb)	1-85937-251-1	£9.99
Preston (pb)	1-85937-212-0	£9.99
Reading (pb)	1-85937-238-4	£9.99
Romford (pb)	1-85937-319-4	£9.99
Salisbury (pb)	1-85937-239-2	£9.99
Scarborough (pb)	1-85937-379-8	£9.99
St Albans (pb)	1-85937-341-0	£9.99
St Ives (pb)	1-85937415-8	£9.99
Scotland (pb)	1-85937-182-5	£9.99
Scottish Castles (pb)	1-85937-323-2	£9.99
Sevenoaks & Tunbridge	1-85937-057-8	£12.99
Sheffield, South Yorks (pb)	1-85937-267-8	£9.99
Shrewsbury (pb)	1-85937-325-9	£9.99
Shropshire (pb)	1-85937-326-7	£9.99
Somerset	1-85937-153-1	£14.99
South Devon Coast	1-85937-107-8	£14.99
South Devon Living Memories	1-85937-168-x	£14.99
South Hams	1-85937-220-1	£14.99
Southampton (pb)	1-85937-427-1	£9.99
Southport (pb)	1-85937-425-5	£9.99
Staffordshire	1-85937-047-0	£12.99
Stratford upon Avon	1-85937-098-5	£12.99
Suffolk (pb)	1-85937-221-x	£9.99
Suffolk Coast	1-85937-259-7	£14.99
Surrey (pb)	1-85937-240-6	£9.99
Sussex (pb)	1-85937-184-1	£9.99
Swansea (pb)	1-85937-167-1	£9.99
Tees Valley & Cleveland	1-85937-211-2	£14.99
Thanet (pb)	1-85937-116-7	£9.99
Tiverton (pb)	1-85937-178-7	£9.99
Torbay	1-85937-063-2	£12.99
Truro	1-85937-147-7	£12.99
Victorian and Edwardian Cornwall	1-85937-252-x	£14.99
Victorian & Edwardian Devon	1-85937-253-8	£14.99
Victorian & Edwardian Kent	1-85937-149-3	£14.99
Vic & Ed Maritime Album	1-85937-144-2	£17.99
Victorian and Edwardian Sussex	1-85937-157-4	£14.99
Victorian & Edwardian Yorkshire	1-85937-154-x	£14.99
Victorian Seaside	1-85937-159-0	£17.99
Villages of Devon (pb)	1-85937-293-7	£9.99
Villages of Kent (pb)	1-85937-294-5	£9.99
Villages of Sussex (pb)	1-85937-295-3	£9.99
Warwickshire (pb)	1-85937-203-1	£9.99
Welsh Castles (pb)	1-85937-322-4	£9.99
West Midlands (pb)	1-85937-289-9	£9.99
West Sussex	1-85937-148-5	£14.99
West Yorkshire (pb)	1-85937-201-5	£9.99
Weymouth (pb)	1-85937-209-0	£9.99
Wiltshire (pb)	1-85937-277-5	£9.99
Wiltshire Churches (pb)	1-85937-171-x	£9.99
Wiltshire Living Memories	1-85937-245-7	£14.99
Winchester (pb)	1-85937-428-x	£9.99
Windmills & Watermills	1-85937-242-2	£17.99
Worcester (pb)	1-85937-165-5	£9.99
Worcestershire	1-85937-152-3	£14.99
York (pb)	1-85937-199-x	£9.99
Yorkshire (pb)	1-85937-186-8	£9.99
Yorkshire Living Memories	1-85937-166-3	£14.99

See Frith books on the internet www.francisfrith.co.uk

FRITH PRODUCTS & SERVICES

Francis Frith would doubtless be pleased to know that the pioneering publishing venture he started in 1860 still continues today. A hundred and forty years later, The Francis Frith Collection continues in the same innovative tradition and is now one of the foremost publishers of vintage photographs in the world. Some of the current activities include:

Interior Decoration

Today Frith's photographs can be seen framed and as giant wall murals in thousands of pubs, restaurants, hotels, banks, retail stores and other public buildings throughout the country. In every case they enhance the unique local atmosphere of the places they depict and provide reminders of gentler days in an increasingly busy and frenetic world.

Product Promotions

Frith products are used by many major companies to promote the sales of their own products or to reinforce their own history and heritage. Frith promotions have been used by Hovis bread, Courage beers, Scots Porage Oats, Colman's mustard, Cadbury's foods, Mellow Birds coffee, Dunhill pipe tobacco, Guinness, and Bulmer's Cider.

Genealogy and Family History

As the interest in family history and roots grows world-wide, more and more people are turning to Frith's photographs of Great Britain for images of the towns, villages and streets where their ancestors lived; and, of course, photographs of the churches and chapels where their ancestors were christened, married and buried are an essential part of every genealogy tree and family album.

Frith Products

All Frith photographs are available Framed or just as Mounted Prints and Posters (size 23 x 16 inches). These may be ordered from the address below. From time to time other products - Address Books, Calendars, Table Mats, etc - are available.

The Internet

Already twenty thousand Frith photographs can be viewed and purchased on the internet through the Frith websites and a myriad of partner sites.

For more detailed information on Frith companies and products, look at these sites:

www.francisfrith.co.uk
www.francisfrith.com
(for North American visitors)

See the complete list of Frith Books at:
www.francisfrith.co.uk
This web site is regularly updated with the latest list of publications from the Frith Book Company. If you wish to buy books relating to another part of the country that your local bookshop does not stock, you may purchase on-line.

For further information, trade, or author enquiries please contact us at the address below:

The Francis Frith Collection, Frith's Barn, Teffont, Salisbury, Wiltshire, England SP3 5QP.
Tel: +44 (0)1722 716 376 Fax: +44 (0)1722 716 881 Email: sales@francisfrith.co.uk

See Frith books on the internet www.francisfrith.co.uk

To receive your FREE Mounted Print

Mounted Print
Overall size 14 x 11 inches

Cut out this Voucher and return it with your remittance for £1.95 to cover postage and handling, to UK addresses. For overseas addresses please include £4.00 post and handling.
Choose any photograph included in this book. Your SEPIA print will be A4 in size, and mounted in a cream mount with burgundy rule line, overall size 14 x 11 inches.

Order additional Mounted Prints at HALF PRICE (only £7.49 each*)
If there are further pictures you would like to order, possibly as gifts for friends and family, purchase them at half price (no additional postage and handling required).

Have your Mounted Prints framed*
For an additional £14.95 per print you can have your chosen Mounted Print framed in an elegant polished wood and gilt moulding, overall size 16 x 13 inches (no additional postage and handling required).

*** IMPORTANT!**
These special prices are only available if ordered using the original voucher on this page (no copies permitted) and at the same time as your free Mounted Print, for delivery to the same address

Frith Collectors' Guild

From time to time we publish a magazine of news and stories about Frith photographs and further special offers of Frith products. If you would like 12 months FREE membership, please return this form.

Send completed forms to:
The Francis Frith Collection, Frith's Barn, Teffont, Salisbury, Wiltshire SP3 5QP

Voucher for FREE and Reduced Price Frith Prints

Picture no.	Page number	Qty	Mounted @ £7.49	Framed + £14.95	Total Cost
		1	**Free of charge***	£	£
			£7.49	£	£
			£7.49	£	£
			£7.49	£	£
			£7.49	£	£
			£7.49	£	£
Please allow 28 days for delivery				*** Post & handling**	**£1.95**
Book Title				**Total Order Cost**	**£**

Please do not photocopy this voucher. Only the original is valid, so please cut it out and return it to us.

I enclose a cheque / postal order for £ ....
made payable to 'The Francis Frith Collection'
OR please debit my Mastercard / Visa / Switch / Amex card
(credit cards please on all overseas orders)

Number ....
Issue No (Switch only) .... Valid from (Amex/Switch) ....
Expires .... Signature ....

Name Mr/Mrs/Ms ....
Address ....
....
....
.... Postcode ....
Daytime Tel No .... Valid to 31/12/03

The Francis Frith Collectors' Guild

Please enrol me as a member for 12 months free of charge.

Name Mr/Mrs/Ms ....
Address ....
....
....
.... Postcode ....

Free Print - see overleaf

Would you like to find out more about Francis Frith?

We have recently recruited some entertaining speakers who are happy to visit local groups, clubs and societies to give an illustrated talk documenting Frith's travels and photographs. If you are a member of such a group and are interested in hosting a presentation, we would love to hear from you.

Our speakers bring with them a small selection of our local town and county books, together with sample prints. They are happy to take orders. A small proportion of the order value is donated to the group who have hosted the presentation. The talks are therefore an excellent way of fundraising for small groups and societies.

Can you help us with information about any of the Frith photographs in this book?

We are gradually compiling an historical record for each of the photographs in the Frith archive. It is always fascinating to find out the names of the people shown in the pictures, as well as insights into the shops, buildings and other features depicted.

If you recognize anyone in the photographs in this book, or if you have information not already included in the author's caption, do let us know. We would love to hear from you, and will try to publish it in future books or articles.

Our production team

Frith books are produced by a small dedicated team at offices in the converted Grade II listed 18th-century barn at Teffont near Salisbury, illustrated above. Most have worked with the Frith Collection for many years. All have in common one quality: they have a passion for the Frith Collection. The team is constantly expanding, but currently includes:

Jason Buck, John Buck, Douglas Burns, Heather Crisp, Lucy Elcock, Isobel Hall, Rob Hames, Hazel Heaton, Peter Horne, James Kinnear, Tina Leary, Hannah Marsh, Eliza Sackett, Terence Sackett, Sandra Sanger, Lewis Taylor, Shelley Tolcher, Helen Vimpany, Clive Wathen and Jenny Wathen.